Pilot's Retire Early

The 9 Critical Decisions When Retiring Before 65

"The Pilot's Advisor"

Ryan J. Fleming, MBA, RICP, CRPC

CONTENTS

WHO AM I?

I was born in central Ohio where the first thing they do is give you a football in the hospital crib, just to ensure there is no confusion about what college football team you will be rooting for. We lived on the outskirts of town in those early years and I remember my father being on the road a lot working various construction projects to make ends meet. My mother took care of my older sister, Ashlee, and I and a few cousins who lived down the street. We spent most of our time playing outside, building forts in the woods and walking up and down the small streams near our house that we referred to as "creekin" later in life.

When I was in first grade, my dad landed a job that got him off the construction projects and we moved away from all my family, venturing south to Cincinnati. He sold plumbing supplies, and this was going to be our new break in life. My parents got a house in a nicer neighborhood that we could hardly afford, and my mom started cleaning houses around town for the more fortunate. It was tough paying the bills, but they were adamant about keeping us in this school district so we could have the opportunity to get a great education.

As soon as I was big enough to start pushing a lawnmower, I started a business cutting grass. That job, combined with my newspaper route, made me feel like I was earning good money; enough to help out around the house and to buy some sports equipment as I started having an interest in all sports.

Although we never went without eating, we lived paycheck to paycheck and were definitely the least fortunate in our town. I decided back then that I was going to work very hard in school so that I would never need to live like that when I grew up. My interest in personal finance, therefore, started early in life.

I excelled in sports and upon graduation, I was being offered football scholarships by many schools in the Big Ten and also the MAC. I knew nothing about the Air Force Academy in Colorado Springs, but after Fisher Deberry, Air Force's Hall of Fame football

Head Coach, showed up at a few of my basketball practices, I agreed to take a visit to Colorado to check it out. Something about it was different and it was one of top educations I could get in the whole country. I graduated with a 3.94, so USAFA was very interested in me. Thankfully, I was being very analytical with my decisions back then because I came home and told my parents that I was going to attend the Air Force Academy, and to this day, I would say that was the single best decision of my life.

The Academy presented a very difficult life and everyone there was extremely intelligent. It was challenging and I met some of the most amazing people there, many of whom became lifelong friends.

I did pretty well in football there, breaking many of the records for wide receivers, and upon graduation, my leadership was trying to figure out a way I could get released from my Air Force commitment so I could play in the NFL. While they worked on that, , I had to give up my pilot training slot because they weren't going to spend millions of dollars on training me to be a pilot so that I could go and play football.

The Secretary of the Air Force eventually said no to this request and playing in the Blue vs Gray All-Star game was the last time I engaged with the sport. I graduated from USAFA with a degree in Business Management in 2001.

After not being released from my active-duty commitment, I served as an Acquisition and Procurement Officer in the United States Air Force. I led a team that negotiated, managed and administered large multi-million-dollar government contracts in the Special Operations world.

I never was totally interested in the military or flying airplanes, but I figured I had the opportunity to try it and I shouldn't pass that up, so I fought to regain my pilot training slot. I still continued to improve myself during this time period and while doing my contracting job, I earned my MBA from the University of Arkansas with a specialization in Human Resource Management.

After a few arduous years of convincing the Air Force that they should send me back to fly, I was selected to attend flight school, and after receiving my wings as an Air Force Pilot, I eventually served multiple tours of duty in Iraq and Afghanistan, flying the mighty C-17A in direct support of the War on Terror.

I loved flying and I love being a part of a crew, but my passion for personal finance never went away. I did quite a bit of self-study courses and reading in the field, but outside of my formal finance classes at the Academy and in accomplishing my MBA, I had no formal education in the field.

I watched many of my buddies make horrible financial decisions as young officers in the Air Force and although I helped many of them, I knew there was a void to be filled.

I've found that in life, everything happens for a reason, despite our best intentions and plans. So, let me tell you how I became a financial advisor.

I was living in Destin, Florida, and I ran into a girl named Kari. I actually knew her before as she was a gorgeous soccer player at the United States Air Force Academy. She was two years younger, but all the guys knew who she was. Kari was extremely intelligent, independent and a very positive person who everyone wanted to be around. I must be very persuasive because I eventually convinced her to marry me and we have been happily married for the past 15 years.

Kari has a great family and eventually, I met her uncle who had been a financial advisor for over 30 years at the time. I would always ask him questions and was constantly picking his brain about this concept or his feelings on that fund. Finally, he convinced me that I would be really great as a financial advisor and he sponsored me to become part of his firm. I studied for months for the financial services version of the "Bar" exam, the Series 7 and the Series 66. The passage rate on these tests was barely 50% and I wanted to make sure I was on the right side of those statistics. Thankfully, I passed both on my first attempt and I left active military service. Then I entered the financial services industry as a Registered Representative for Cantella & Company, a SEC registered Broker/Dealer, located in the financial district of Boston.

After building my practice for a few years, I learned so much more about the business and knew the best thing for my clients and their future was to start my own firm and become a fiduciary.

As a fiduciary, I would be legally obligated to act in my client's best interest at all times and I would no longer need to deal with the products that the broker dealer was pushing. I studied so many very successful financial advisors, but I wasn't convinced they were truly doing what was best for their clients. I was going to change that. In 2009, the Fleming Financial Group, LLC was founded. I now had my own RIA.

Over the years, I earned a few more certifications and became a trusted name and advisor for the military community and fellow commercial pilots. This is how I eventually became known as the "Pilot's Advisor."

I take great pride in helping my fellow aviators invest their money in a responsible and prudent manner. I don't want to just manage their money, instead, I want to educate and teach them to stop speculating and gambling with their money. I teach them about how to use Nobel Prize winning research and academics to make investment decisions versus trying to predict the future. I teach them how to find true investment peace of mind so that they can sleep at night. I teach them how to "own and trust" a long-term investment philosophy.

My firm has grown considerably over the years and I look forward to one day running it with my wife Kari when she leaves active military service. She is currently a Commander of a C-17 Squadron at Charleston Air Force base where we currently reside with our two children, Jaden and Race, and our yellow lab, Chuck.

WHY AREN'T MORE PILOT'S ABLE TO RETIRE BEFORE 65?

From my years in the financial industry, I have realized there is one major issue. The major issue is most Wall Street advisors are out of touch with the needs of their clients and end up leaving their clients' money in high-risk investments. They say things like, "You're in this for the long haul. It's only a paper loss," you've probably heard those lines before. They also overcharge in fees and make things way too complicated, thinking that it makes them look smarter. Most advisors are focused on accumulating money and never think about the huge impact of clients losing hundreds of thousands of dollars in retirement. Not being this type of advisor has motivated me over the years to be the best advisor I can be for my fellow pilots.

Too Focused on the Small Picture

Most Wall Street firms are overly focused on investments, when, investments are only a small part of what you must worry about in retirement. What about Social Security options? When do you take your Social Security? What about taxes? Why aren't they looking at the future and addressing the big picture?

When I speak to my clients the number one feeling I sense across the board is fear. It comes in many different words. Some people are anxious. Some people are worried. Some people are concerned. But at the end of the day, fear is fear. And fear of the future is the worst fear you can feel.

Unfortunately, most financial advisors aren't very helpful in relieving that fear, most are so busy trying to make a commission, fees and revenues that they're not diving deeper into your problems, your needs and your concerns. They're not taking the time to listen to you.

They need to know, what keeps you up at night? What makes you anxious? Is it a long life in retirement? Is it taxes? Is it making sure you provide for the next generation? I think those topics are important and need to be addressed and evaluated, because those concerns and anxieties can be alleviated.

At the end of the day, if you don't answer the questions that worry you, you're going to live a long life in retirement being more concerned about your finances instead of being with your grandkids and enjoying your vacation. Finding financial peace of mind is the ultimate goal so that you can enjoy your retirement.

My Hope for You

What I hope you get from reading this book, is a solution. My desire for you is to see that investments, while important, will not be the main reason you succeed in retirement. If you truly want to succeed in retirement, you need a comprehensive plan to alleviate your fears.

Your plan should be multi-dimensional, but at the same time it should be simple, and easy to understand. The plan needs to take into account your income along with inflation to ensure you have enough money to last throughout retirement.

Another dimension of your plan, if you're married, should include provisions for the surviving spouse to live the rest of their life, if one of you passes away. Also, you must have a Social Security plan which would include the best time to take Social Security.

When we have alleviated your fear around all those topics, we can look at your investment plan. We want to make sure you're not taking more risk than you're comfortable with, and that your investments have grown to keep pace with inflation.

Lastly the most important part of looking at your investments is to be sure if there is a market decline, you won't lose half your portfolio.

Creating Your Plan

Now let's take a look at what it means to create your plan. Your plan should definitely include taxes. Taxes are one of the things, in my opinion, that are the number one threat for retirees, even more so than market decline. The greedy tax man wants to steal your hard-earned money.

The government has a tax lien against your retirement!

I talk to pilots all the time who think all that money in their 401k is theirs. "Hell yeah, that's my money!" Nope, you have entered into a partnership with the US Gov't and with the stroke of a pen, they can take an even higher percentage of that money!

Most people don't realize the threat they are facing from the government. For example, if you needed $1,000 out of your portfolio but you were in the 30% combined tax bracket, you're going to have to take out $1,400 to get the $1,000 back.

Over time, that can raise the risk of you running out of money, even more so than the stock market decline. Also, from a tax standpoint, it's not only the taxes you must pay from your portfolio.

If you don't have the appropriate plan, it can also raise the taxes on your Social Security. It could raise the cost of your Medicare, and if this government decides to raise taxes, it can put an even bigger dent in your portfolio. Taxes are a huge concern for retirees; we need a plan to alleviate that.

Healthcare

The next big concern for retirees is healthcare. Retiring before 65 could mean you must pick up COBRA or private health insurance. Many times, I've heard my clients say they have avoided early retirement not because they don't have enough money, but because they're concerned about the healthcare cost. If you didn't retire from the military, you will have to bridge the gap from 60-65.

Here's the thing. Healthcare doesn't stop at making sure you have the proper health insurance choice. You also must consider a possible future need for long term care. In my state, of South Carolina, the average cost of in-home care is about $90,000 per year. Just imagine $90,000 a year and the impact that can have on a person's portfolio, even if you had the perfect plan. Many clients are shocked to realize their health insurance does not cover long-term care. Your health insurance only covers 90 days. So, it's very important to have a long-term comprehensive plan in place to make sure it doesn't wipe away all the retirement savings.

Planning Your Legacy

Finally, we need to create a plan for your legacy. We must make sure you haven't taken all this time building up your net worth, and then God forbid if you pass away, your heirs must go through probate. We want to make sure you at least have a conversation about a trust or a will. We want to make sure your heirs won't have half of their assets taken away due to the greedy tax man coming after their inheritance.

I want you to understand, to have a successful retirement, you need a plan that covers those five critical areas, and you need someone you can trust to help you with that. I believe I am that person.

CRITICAL DECISION NUMBER ONE

WHERE WILL MY INCOME COME FROM?

One of the most important decisions you'll make before you retire is, how much income will you need for retirement? We don't want you to merely survive in retirement. We want you to thrive in retirement that's why it's so important to have an income plan.

Dan's Story

Let me give you an example. I had a client who came in. We'll call him Dan. Dan sat down next to me, and we had a conversation about how much he spent per month. Dan said, "Well, I only spend about $2,000 per month. All I'll need in retirement is about $2,000 per month."

Granted, he did have a low house note. I think his house note was only about $800 per month. However, as we began to talk and I dug deeper into his lifestyle, his concerns, his worries, and his needs, it became harder to believe that Dan only needed $2,000 per month.

He told me about his spouse's shopping habits. He also began to tell me about how much he loved to golf. Now, if Dan is anything like me, golf is a very expensive sport. Most of my balls end up in the water or the trees, so I know that can catch up with you quickly.

I said, "Hey Dan, would you mind if we took 15 minutes to go through a spending plan with you to see if we can build it around $2,000 a month?" He said, "Yep." As we began to dig deeper, I found quite a few expenses he hadn't mentioned. Not only was he paying the $800 mortgage that he expected to pay off in a few years, but he was also paying off a student loan for his son at $600 per month. As it turned out, I was correct about the golfing habit. He spends $400 per month to belong to a golf organization. Also, I discovered he was helping his mom for about $400 per month.

All of that was before we discussed other interests and expenses like travel and utilities. It turns out those expenses added up to over $2,500 of "fixed expenses" he had to pay. Once we got his travel needs and the rest of his goals and how much he ate out, it kept adding up.

Let's talk for a moment about food. That's something you can't live without. He was also spending $800 a month for a meal service company that prepared meals for him. I can understand why. Sometimes I don't want to cook either!

It turns out that his expenses were about $5,500 per month. That's a little bit more than $2,000. Once we found out that his actual expenses were $5,500, we looked at his income sources. It turns out for Dan and his spouse, their income sources included about $2,000 for a pension and $1,500 for his spouse's Social Security. He received no Social Security, which left us with an income gap of over $2,000 that we needed to fill per month, not including taxes.

How Much Do You *Really* Spend?

The most important thing you can do is get clarity on exactly how much money you're spending in retirement. Sometimes it helps to make a budget worksheet, but when you make the budget worksheet, don't think about what you're spending out of necessity. Think about what your short-term goals are, and your long-term goals as well. Is it spending time with the grandkids? Is it traveling? Is it playing more golf? There are things you can do to still meet all your goals and at the same time make sure you don't run out of money in retirement.

And let's not forget, we also must consider inflation. When we build a retirement income plan for you, we don't look at the income you have now. We also need to look at the income projected at a 3% inflation rate. That's the first critical decision that needs to be made.

Here's the important part. Once you realize what your income gap is, the next thing you need to do is devise a plan of where you will take that money from. There will be a need to take income from your portfolio. You want to make sure you're not overly aggressive in the withdrawals from the account that you're counting on for income, for the rest of your life.

CRITICAL DECISION NUMBER TWO

SHOULD I REDUCE MY RISK?

One of my early clients, we'll call her Marsha, was a 63-year-old widow, recently retired. She came into our office and asked us to help her make sure part of her portfolio was safe. She was at a point in her life where she could not deal with the market risk. She could not deal with the ups and downs and it was causing her too much anxiety. It was literally causing her to lose sleep.

We helped her devise a plan that was based on a more conservative model, which she was very pleased with. She thought for sure we were about to have a market correction. By the way, she was right. A market correction did follow. It seemed to start the very next week, so I don't know if she's a psychic or what, but she was right.

Unfortunately, after we devised the conservative plan, she called me about two days later, following a conversation with her son. She mentioned to me that her son, who was 28, asked her why she would want to reduce her risk when the market had been doing so well. This son convinced her not to adopt a more conservative plan. Instead, he convinced her to go in the opposite direction with a different advisor, which was to be even more aggressive.

Her portfolio started at about $600,000. She ended up losing $300,000 when the market declined. Do you think her son refunded her the $300,000 she lost because of his advice? Probably not.

When a client comes into my office and shows me their portfolio, 80% of the time, they tell me they don't want to take too much risk, but almost always, when I look at their portfolio, they're at more risk than they thought. Therefore, for every client, we do a stress test portfolio to determine if they're taking too much risk. One of the things we always want to know is, how much are you comfortable losing if we have a bad market decline. If the market went down, what is the highest percentage you would be willing to lose? It's a scary question, but an important one to answer.

How Much are You Willing to Lose?

Let's say a person told me, "The most I'll be willing to lose is 20%." If we stress-test their portfolio and it shows there have been several times when their portfolio lost more than 45%, then it's probable that person is taking too much risk.

One of the easiest ways to tell if you're taking too much risk is to follow a simple rule called the rule of 100. To follow this rule, you take the number 100 and subtract it by your age. If you're 62, 100 minus 62 is 38. That means no more than 38% of your portfolio should be at too much risk, 62% should probably be safer.

Now, that's not for everybody, but for a typical person who is taking income from their portfolio, that is the standard rule of thumb. If you don't need income from your portfolio, it could potentially be a reverse, so it depends on your situation.

I always recommend my clients get a review of their portfolio to determine that they won't end up like my grandmother. When the market declined, she lost half of her money, causing her to run out of money.

SHOULD PAY OFF MY HOUSE

A nother of the critical concern's clients have before retirement is debt. Sometimes they have credit card debt or maybe vehicle debt. They might have student loan debt they're paying out for their child. I get a lot of clients who believe they cannot retire unless they pay off the mortgage, and that couldn't be further from the truth.

Greg's Story

Greg and Sandy both retired. They were 61 years old; Greg wanted to pull money out of his Thrift Savings Plan to pay off the house. He had $275,000 in a Thrift Savings Plan, and there was about $150,000 pay off. The problem with that is, if Greg took the $150,000 out, he would, of course, pay taxes on the money as well. Here's the crazy part he has to pay taxes on that $150,000 which means he could potentially pull out $200,000 to pay off the house of $150,000. Not only does he pay taxes on the withdrawn money, now he put himself in a higher tax bracket.

Even though he was gung-ho about doing this, at least he called me so we could talk it over. I was able to talk him emotionally through that decision, and one of the things I told him was, "If you spend down this Thrift Savings Plan and pay the taxes, you will miss out on any gains if the market were to come back up." Thankfully, he followed my advice and decided to continue paying extra on the house and still was able to retire.

One of the most fantastic moments of my career was seven years later when Greg called me and said, "I want to thank you so much, Ryan, for all the help you gave me and for keeping me from making a big mistake." He said, "Not only did I make my last payment for the home this month, but I also have $350,000 in my Thrift Savings Plan, which is even more than I had before I came to you." That was one of the most rewarding moments of my life because it made me realize the advice I give on a day to day basis we truly does help people and changes lives.

When it Makes Sense to Pay Off the House

Now, there are some situations where you're not getting an interest deduction on your house, and you have a $30,000 mortgage, but you also have money sitting in cash not doing anything for you. In those cases, sure, it might make sense to pay off the house, but there's typically the logical side and the emotional side. The logical side might say it's better to keep the mortgage and pay it out over time, but it's that emotional side which causes you anxiety where you can't stomach the debt, where you listen to your grandmother's advice about not keeping the debt.

If that anxiety is keeping you up at night to the point you can't concentrate on enjoying your retirement, in that case, even though it may not make logical sense, it still might make sense to pay off the house. My advice is to make sure you sit down with a professional and analyze your options before you make a huge tax mistake you can't recover from.

WHEN SHOULD I TAKE SOCIAL SECURITY?

Social Security is one of the key decisions to be made when deciding to retire early. My biggest problem with a lot of investment gurus and TV talking heads is they'll give you a blanket statement like, "Oh, it's always best to take Social Security later in life, because it continues to defer. You continue to get 8% credits per year," or you get the opposite advice from some radio and TV talking heads who say you always should take Social Security early, because you need to enjoy every moment you can and spend it down. The reality of it is it's a gray area.

A $30,000 Mistake

I'll give you an example of a client who made a $30,000+ Social Security mistake. He was the person who said, "No matter what, I will always take my Social Security early," so he retired at 62 and began to take his Social Security at 62. As he was taking his Social Security, he realized he was bored in retirement and wanted to go back to work, so he accepted a part-time job that was paying him $80,000 per year part-time. That's a pretty great part-time job. I probably would've gone back to work myself!

This client was already taking Social Security, so when he sat down with me for the first time, he didn't realize what was happening to his benefits. His Social Security was more than $28,000 per year. Now, because of his income of $80,000, for every dollar he made above $17,000, there was a 50% penalty on his Social Security because he took it early, before his full retirement age. Because of that, he owed the IRS $31,000 in penalties.

Now, if I'd had an opportunity to talk to him beforehand, I would have made sure he was ready to retire before he started to take his Social Security fully.

Once you turn full retirement age, which, for some people, is between 66 and 67, you're allowed to make as much money as you want without incurring any Social Security penalties. It's only if you choose to take Social Security earlier that you get penalized.

To Delay or Not to Delay?

On the other hand, I had a couple, age 62 and 63, who always thought they should delay their Social Security benefits no matter what. They had about $500,000 in their retirement account. They had no pension. They needed $50,000 per year to live on. To delay their Social Security benefits, they decided to take the money from their portfolio until they reached the age of full retirement. Well, in this instance, they were taking out over $50,000 per year from a $500,000 account. If you do the math, you'll realize that's 10% per year. They may not even make it to full retirement age before they run out of money at that rate. Imagine a market decline happening while they're taking over 10% of their portfolio. Now, at least they didn't go back to work and incur any penalties, but still, it wasn't in their best interest to delay their Social Security. They should have met with a qualified advisor like me to do a Social Security analysis.

More than likely, it would have been determined that at least one of them should have taken their Social Security benefits and maybe the other spouse should have delayed it. In some cases, maybe they both should've started their Social Security benefits.

It's a gray area. There are more than 400 different ways you can take Social Security. There are spousal benefits and other things you need to know. Don't think you can call the Social Security Administration and get advice. They're not trained to give you strategies. They can only tell you the facts. Even then, when you call three different times, you might get three different answers. It pays to sit down and truly evaluate their advice.

SHOULD I ROLLOVER MY 401(K)?

Most people are concerned about this critical decision because it's the most common decision. You leave a job. You've been used to accumulating money for all these years. You know the company is safe. By the way, contributing to the 401(k) is what got you to where you are now, so why should you move it?

There's a reason most people move their 401(k) and roll it over into an IRA when they retire. Most 401(k) s have limited investment options. When you retire, you can no longer contribute to that 401(k). Typically, nobody's watching that, and you don't have any control over that retirement plan. In some cases, they can change the company without your permission because you have no say-so or any voting rights.

By rolling over your retirement plan, you get an opportunity, if you still work, to contribute to that retirement plan still, but more importantly, you can take control of how you invest that money.

Be Careful

Don't take a withdrawal with your name on it thinking you're going to roll it over. You want to make sure that it's written to an institution for the benefit of you. If you write it in your name, it becomes a taxable event. You want to avoid any taxable events like that.

There are some cases where I recommend a person keep their 401(k), or at least a portion of their 401(k), in their retirement plan. If you're retiring early, even before the age of 59 1/2, there is a critical rule you need to know. If you retire after 55, you're able to have access to that 401(k) without a penalty. Typically, there's a 10% penalty if you take money out of your retirement account before you're 59 1/2. That's one of the exceptions. If you leave a company in the year in which you turn 55 or older, even if you haven't reached that age of 59 1/2, you're able to take money out of that portfolio without a penalty. That might give you some flexibility and control, especially if you need the money from that retirement plan.

Proceed with Caution

Be careful of some Wall Street Brokers who will try to convince you to roll over all that money to them no matter what. Once you make a mistake and roll over that 401(k) to an IRA, that decision is final. You cannot go back and revert it. You cannot touch that account until you're 59 1/2 without a penalty unless you enact a certain rule.

We won't talk too much about it, but there's a rule called 72-T where you can take substantial payments, but you must continue to do so over five years. You're forced to do it, or they will go back and penalize all your previous withdrawals. Let's try to avoid that and make sure you're getting good, qualified advice when it comes to rolling over your 401(k).

There's one extra rule you need to know about. Let's say you're still working, and you hit the age of 59 1/2. Even though you're still working, you're eligible to roll over that money into an IRA. It's called an in-service distribution, which means that, even while you're in service and still working, you could still roll that money over.

The reason why your company allows you to do so is they realize that more 401(k)s are focused on the accumulation stage of preparing for retirement, and they don't have a lot of options for people who are moving closer to retirement and their distribution stage.

SHOULD I CHOOSE A LUMP SUM PENSION?

There was a time in the glory days, when a person could retire after working 40 years, they'd get a gold watch, a nice pension, and Social Security. Best of all they'd be able to take money from their assets. It was called the three-legged stool. Those days are almost gone. Most companies are not even offering pensions. They're making you contribute to your retirement plan, which is the 401(k). Sure, they might give you a match, if that, but the pension decision becomes a little more complicated and a little more difficult.

Now, there are still companies that provide you with a pension, but some also provide you the choice to take it monthly or in a lump sum. The factors to consider when determining if you should take your pension lump sum is, number one, do you need the income? Do you need all the income? If you don't need all the income, at first glance, it might seem like, "Well, I might as well take it monthly, because I don't need it, so I'll have more than enough income."

The challenge with taking a pension monthly is, if you're taking more income than you need, you're going to have to pay taxes on that extra money. If you don't need that extra money and you pay taxes on it, more than likely, you're going to put that extra money into a taxable account, which means you're going to have to pay compounded taxes on that money again. If you don't need the income, it makes sense to control your income and take the lump sum pension.

Cost of Living

Another factor to consider is if your pension has a cost-of-living adjustment? If you're receiving $2,000 a month now on a pension, but in 20 years, it's still only $2,000 per month, that $2,000 per month might only feel like $500 a month. Inflation continues to rise, but your income stays the same.

Sometimes people decide to do a lump sum pension because they're able to grow their money with inflation, and they're able to increase their income over time.

Another reason a person might consider a lump sum pension is they want their heirs to get that money when they pass away. Some of the downsides of the pension income strategy are, if your spouse passes away and you pass away, your kids get absolutely nothing.

Unfortunately, I had an experience with one of my clients who took his pension as a monthly income, he chose a single life where his spouse got zero when he passed away, and God forbid, one year later he passed away in a car accident and lost everything. If he had taken the lump sum pension, it would have been over $550,000. Because he didn't choose a lump sum, the money went back to the company.

That's a factor you need to consider. If the spread is so far between the monthly income and what you think you can get a lump sum, sometimes it does make sense to take the monthly option, but again, these decisions need to be evaluated by a professional advisor.

One of the recommendations I'll give you is not to put your lump sum pension in too much risk. If that money was meant for income and the market goes down, and you lose up to 40% of your money, you've lost the money that was supposed to be focused on your long-term income security. Make sure, when you're making that decision, you're getting the professional help you need. As part of our dream retirement process, we help you evaluate, among other things, the best lump sum, the best pension option, as well as the best ways to take Social Security and protect your portfolio.

CRITICAL DECISION NUMBER SEVEN

WHAT SHOULD I DO ABOUT HEALTH INSURANCE?

As I mentioned earlier, health insurance is one of the main worries for most retirees, especially those retiring early. They think about the fact they have an income gap so if they retire at 60, they have five years before Medicare comes into play. How do they fill that gap?

Don't Get Bit by COBRA

One of the ways to fill that gap is for one spouse to continue working so their job will cover the health insurance under the family plan. This is one of the most common things I see people do, but if you both must retire, my advice would be not to think that COBRA is going to be your only solution. I've found, time and time again, that health insurance can be cheaper in an open market than is offered on your COBRA. On average, a person spends $600 per month on COBRA, and it may or may not meet your needs.

Another thing to consider is your Medicare supplement plan. Once you turn 63, people begin to call you like vultures. You begin to get all these random phone calls you may get 100 different documents in the mail. Everybody is trying to tell you they have the best Medicare supplement plan on earth.

How do you pick the right plan when you have so many people giving you conflicting advice? It's almost impossible, which is why I recommend you sit down with an independent Medicare specialist. Our company has an independent Medicare specialist who meets with our clients to give them several different competitive prices, with no real conflict of interest in which company you choose. I think that's extremely important when making that Medicare decision. I strongly recommend you at least look at a supplement, because we don't want a medical situation to happen where you owe $20,000 you didn't anticipate paying.

Long-Term Care

The other thing we must consider is long-term care. Long-term care is one of the biggest threats that can wipe out your retirement accounts, no matter how great your investment plan is. There is a 70% chance one person in a married couple will need long-term care at some point in their life.

When you think about long-term care, I know the first thing you think about is a nursing home, but actually, most long-term care policies are meant to keep you out of a nursing home, not to put you in a nursing home. This is one of the things I wish my grandmother had known. If she had a long-term care policy, she would not have run out of money, and maybe I wouldn't be writing this book, because I might not be in this industry. It's one of those situations where it was a blessing in disguise for my career, but I wish things could have ended up differently for my grandmother.

Take a moment and think about people you know who are sick, maybe your parents or someone else you know, who had to go into a long-term care facility or have in-home care. Think about the damages that did to their financial situation. This is a real threat and something that absolutely should be addressed by every financial advisor. When it comes to long-term care you want solutions that will compliment your plan to have a long life in retirement.

Tough Decisions

I remember one of my clients was able to get approved for a long-term care policy, it was one of those things she almost didn't do because of the premium involved with it. After much consideration, she decided to go ahead and do it. Unfortunately, three years later, she developed dementia. As her health continued to get worse, her family had to make the tough decision to put her into an assisted living facility. The assisted living facility cost her $65,000 per year, which is inexpensive for assisted living comparisons. However, her portfolio was worth only about $400,000.

She lived seven years in that assisted living facility before she passed away. If she hadn't bought plan, I can't help but think how devastating that would have been to her financially. She probably would have had to spend down her assets below $1,000 to qualify for Medicaid. I'm sure she probably would have felt like she was a burden on her family.

Those are some of the times I can look at it and see that it really paid off to make sure there was a plan in place. Even if you must self-insure, have a plan.

No Cookie Cutter Plans

Every client I speak to has a different set of circumstances, beliefs and funds available to them. Just like there are a variety of people and lifestyles. There are several different ways to pay for long-term care. The traditional way is old-fashioned premiums, but nowadays, there are things you can do, such as getting an insurance policy with a long-term care rider. That means that, if you ever had a long-time-care-qualifying incident, you would be able to accelerate and spend down your death benefit early, tax-free. If you never use it, your heirs get all the money as a death benefit.

There are also asset-based ways to pay for long-term care insurance. I had a client who had $200,000, and I asked her why she had so much in cash. She said, "Just in case an emergency happens." When I drilled down deeper, I found out that the emergency she was talking about was health. We were able to take $100,000 of that and leverage it into an asset-based long-term care plan where, if she needed long-term care, her long-term care benefit would multiply by four times that $100,000 amount, tax-free. If she changed her mind, she could always take her $100,000 back. If she passed away, the money plus some interest would go to her beneficiary. Just know that you are not stuck with the old traditional way of long-term care, but it's something every person who decides to retire early should consider.

CRITICAL DECISION NUMBER EIGHT

WHAT ABOUT TAXES?

One of the biggest threats to retirement security that no one is talking about is the impact taxes could have on your retirement. Most retirees spent their entire working careers contributing money to their IRAs, 401(k) s, 403(b) s, Thrift Savings Plans, and other tax-deferred accounts because they were told that if you get a deduction right now, you won't need the deduction later. Defer your taxes and pay the taxes later, because you'll be making less income.

"Want to" Versus "Have to"

The problem is, for most people, that's not true because they want to. It could be true because they must. Now, statistically speaking, yes, it's true people spend less than 70%, but it's because they have no choice because they haven't saved enough money. I prefer my clients to maintain their lifestyle instead of taking a pay cut. How do you do so with the danger of taxes? When you retire, and you pull money out of those taxed accounts, you must pay taxes on everything. I call this the *ticking tax time bomb.* It's the ticking tax bomb because, at any moment, it could explode.

What If...

What if the Government Decides to Raise Taxes? What if you have an emergency and you need to take more money out of your account, and it bumps you into a higher tax bracket? What about being forced to take money out of your retirement account once you turn 72? It's called required minimum distributions. What about when you pass away? What happens to all that tax-deferred money? Your heirs would have to pay taxes on all that money over time at their highest tax bracket, which could be a higher income level than you have, as well as, at a higher tax rate.

How do you avoid that retirement tax bomb? One of the things in any plan that we need to determine is if it makes sense to begin to convert some of your tax-deferred money to tax-free money, utilizing tools such as a Roth IRA.

Granted, when you take money from an IRA or a 401(k) and move it into a Roth, you do pay taxes now, but does it make more sense to pay the taxes now while taxes are less expensive, or does it make more sense to wait until taxes potentially go up?

Our country, at the time of this book's writing, is over $28 trillion in debt. We are currently at one of the lowest tax brackets our country has ever seen. With the entitlements, with our debt, with the fact that Social Security could be in some trouble before 2035, eventually, the government's going to have to find a way to pay for this. How do you think they're going to pay for it? You guessed it, potentially increasing taxes.

What if we could find a way to convert most of your money to a tax-free bucket so that, when required minimum distributions come at 70 1/2, you won't have to pay as many taxes, and in some cases, it's possible for you to retire completely tax-free? If we could help you do that, wouldn't you want to know about it? That's a critical decision that could cure an even bigger threat than potential stock market decline.

HOW DO I CHOOSE AN ADVISOR?

When you're looking for an advisor to help you with a comprehensive, critical overview, you must make sure the advisor is a fiduciary. Fiduciary means the advisor must do what's in your best interest. They don't have the conflict of interest of getting commissions like most Wall Street advisors. You would be surprised to know that most advisors are not fiduciaries. Most advisors are not legally required to do what's in your best interest or legally required to do what's in their company's best interest.

Accumulation Versus Distribution

The second thing you must look for is, make sure the broker or advisor is focused on the distribution stage versus the accumulation stage. It's a different planning concept. When you're accumulating your money, you don't have to worry about taxes, healthcare, Social Security or any of those things. You must worry about trying to grow your money as quickly as possible.

I would always ask a financial advisor his average client's age. If his average client's age isn't in your demographic, that may not be the advisor who is most prepared to help you.

Are They Independent?

Are they forced to follow the orders of the company, or are they forced to do what's right for you? Do they supply company, cookie-cutter investment plans, or do they take time to listen to your situation and determine your needs? Are they patient, do they give you customized advice based on your situation, not based on what the company tells them to do?

Focus Focus Focus

Finally, what is their focus? I always want to know if a financial advisor focuses on comprehensive financial advice or if they focus on a product. You can get an insurance agent or even a stockbroker who can pose as a comprehensive financial advisor, but I'd always want to know what's most important to you. Do they focus more on the plan, do they focus more on income, or are they so busy trying to focus and push the latest annuity or the latest stock to you they lose focus that you need help on an overall, comprehensive view? These are very important questions. You should never feel uncomfortable asking your advisor these questions; they owe it to you to provide you with answers.

OUR INVESTMENT PHILOSOPHY

Our investment philosophy is that we cannot give you solid advice, unless we take the time to get to know you, and to understand your unique situation. We also have a philosophy that your plan should be about more than your investments. Your investments are only a piece of the puzzle, so we must look at the five critical areas. Those critical areas are income, investments, taxes, legacy, and healthcare.

Keep it Simple

We believe in keeping things simple and easy to understand. We believe, if an advisor is giving you information that is too complex and you don't understand it, they're trying to prove how smart they are, and that doesn't serve your best interest. Many of our clients are surprised at the level of ease with which we can take them through their retirement process. I've have heard from so many of my clients that for the first time ever they now understand what they are looking at when they look over their portfolio and financial statements.

Slow and Steady Wins

We also believe in conservative strategies. Our best clients are the ones who want to make sure they're going to be okay in the end. When they first meet with us they may have a little bit of anxiety or worry, but they want to fix those worries and anxieties. They don't care about making the highest returns in the shortest amount of time possible. They care about making sure they have the best advice that's going to make their money last, and that they're going to be okay in retirement.

Finally, we believe in the process. We don't believe that everything should be handled in one meeting. We believe we should take things a bit slower. We aren't in a rush, and the most important thing in our relationship is we understand your situation. With that knowledge, we will be able to build you a well-designed process to handle all the priority issues. When we have taken the time to get to know your goals and dreams of the future, it is then we are equipped to find the best plan to approach your priorities.

We believe this knowledge will guide us in creating a process that will take you through the five critical areas of retirement planning: income planning, investment planning, tax planning, healthcare planning, and legacy planning. We would love the opportunity to meet with you.

OUR UNIQUE PROCESS

I want to share a short version of our process with you. As I said earlier, we like to take it slow. If you are interested in working with us, you should have the preliminary information to review.

Once you come in for a meeting, we will sit down and go over some pointed questions to be assured we are a good fit to work with each other. We share our basic beliefs with you to determine if we are on the same page. We must have some simple agreements. You must have realistic expectations for returns. You must be okay with us keeping it simple and easy to understand. You must be a little more conservative and not so tied to an advisor that you are not willing to consider a change.

We then dive into the investment accounts to see if there are any red flags. Red flags could be too much risk, fees, too much money in cash, not keeping pace with inflation, not enough of an emergency fund, no income protection, a previous 401(k) at another company, an advisor who is not a fiduciary or with whom they don't have a great relationship, too many taxes, etc.

We then look at your income now and what you expect to receive in retirement as well as expected expenses. We look at debt you may have and any emergency funds. From there, we determine if it makes sense to pay off debt or pay off the house and how we can fill that income gap.

The next step is to design. We design an income retirement plan and strategy together that's going to help you fulfill your needs. If everything makes sense, and if we're on the same page, the last step is to implement. Of course, we continue with ongoing services which do not stop for as long as you're a client. If this plan sounds like something that would be of benefit to you, please make an appointment so we can talk about it, I look forward to speaking with you.

ARE YOU PLANNING TO RETIRE BEFORE 65? THERE ARE CRITICAL DECISIONS YOU MUST MAKE BEFORE TAKING THE LEAP INTO RETIREMENT

T oo many times, I have spoken with clients who, on the suggestion of friends, relatives, and well-meaning advisors, jump into retirement without proper planning. Too many times, I have had the unpleasant experience of sharing with them the tax consequences of their decisions.

Inside this book, you will learn the Critical Decisions you must make before you retire. Whether Social Security is a concern, Pension Planning, or 401(k)s, all your hard-earned money can be at risk if Critical Decisions are not made at the proper time.

Here's where I come in. I can help you plan for your upcoming retirement. If you find the information in this book to be of value and you would like to learn more, here's what you do next:

Step 1: Go to our website, **www.flemingfg.com** download your free "Retirement Rescue Kit" or email us and request one.

Step 2: If you are interested in working with us, call **843-475-3038** to set up a complimentary 15-minute appointment.

Feel free to email me with any questions: **ryan@flemingfg.com**.

You have worked hard your entire life to ensure you and your family are well taken care of during your retirement. Let's make sure your plans work out the way you've always dreamed.

Ryan J. Fleming, MBA, RICP, CRPC

"The Pilot's Advisor"

www.pilotsadvisor.com

APPENDICES

APPENDIX I

THE ROTH 401(K)

Under a regular 401(k), 403(b), or 457(b) governmental plan, a participant chooses to defer a portion of his or her compensation into the plan. Such "elective deferrals" are made on a pre-tax basis, any account growth is tax- deferred, and withdrawals are taxed as ordinary income.[1]

In a qualified Roth contribution program, a participant can choose to have all or part of his or her elective deferrals made to a separate, designated Roth account. Such "designated Roth contributions" are made on an after-tax basis. Growth in the

designated Roth account is tax-deferred and qualified distributions are excluded from gross income.

---

[1] The discussion here concerns federal income tax law. State or local income tax law may differ.

Other point

- Separate accounting and recordkeeping are required for the deferrals under the regular, pre-tax portions of a plan and for those made to the after-tax, designated Roth account.

- Individuals whose adjusted gross income exceeds certain limits may not contribute to a regular Roth IRA. There are no such income limits applicable to a designated Roth account.

- For 401(k) plans, contributions to a designated Roth account are elective deferrals for purposes of the Actual Deferral Percentage (ADP) test.

CONTRIBUTIONS

A number of rules apply to contributions to a qualified Roth contribution program:

- **Dollar limitation:** For 2020, a maximum of $19,500 may be contributed. Those who are age 50 and older may make additional contributions of $6,500. A participant may choose to place all of his or her contributions in the regular, pre-tax portion of a plan, all in the designated Roth account, or split the deferrals between the two.

- Employer contributions: Employer contributions will be credited only to the regular, pre-tax portion of a plan they may not be designated as Roth contributions.

- **Excess contributions:** Excess deferrals to a designated Roth account must be distributed to the participant no later than April 15 of the year following the year in which the excess deferral was made. Otherwise, the excess deferral will be taxed twice, once in the year of deferral and a second time the year a corrective distribution is made.

DISTRIBUTIONS

A distribution from a designated Roth account will be excluded from income if it is made at least five years after a contribution to such an account was first made and at least one of the following applies:

- The participant reaches age 59½;
- The participant dies;
- The participant becomes disabled.

Such distributions are known as "qualified" distributions.

Other points

Nonqualified distributions: If a distribution does not meet the above requirements, it is termed a "nonqualified" distribution. Such distributions are subject to federal income tax, including a 10% premature distribution penalty if the participant is under age 59½ in the year the funds are distributed. Such distributions are taxed under the annuity rules of IRC Sec. 72; any part of a distribution that is attributable to earnings is includable in income; any portion attributable to the original investment (basis) is recovered tax-free. This contrasts sharply with the taxation of nonqualified distributions from a regular Roth IRA account. Nonqualified distributions from a regular Roth IRA are taxed following pre-defined ordering rules under which basis is recovered first, followed by earnings.

- **First-time homebuyer expenses:** In a regular Roth IRA, a qualified distribution may be made to pay for first-time homebuyer expenses. This provision does not apply to distributions from a designated Roth account.

- **Rollovers to designated Roth accounts:** Distributions from the regular, pre-tax portion of a qualified plan may be rolled-over into a designated Roth account. The individual (either the participant or a surviving spouse) must include the distribution in gross income (subject to basis recovery) in the same manner as if the distribution from the pre-tax plan had been rolled over into a Roth IRA.

- **Rollovers from designated Roth accounts:** A distribution from a designated Roth account may only be rolled over into a Roth IRA or another designated Roth account. Such a rollover is not a taxable event

- **Required minimum distributions:** Generally, amounts in a designated Roth account are subject to the required minimum distribution rules applicable to plan participants when they reach age 72. However, a participant can avoid the mandated distributions by rolling over amounts in the designated Roth account into a regular Roth IRA.

Ryan J. Fleming, MBA, RICP, CRPC

WHICH ACCOUNT TO CHOOSE?

The decision as to which type of account should be used will generally be made on factors such as the length of time until retirement (or until the funds are needed), the amount of money available to contribute each year, the participant's current tax situation, and the anticipated marginal tax rate in retirement. An important issue to keep in mind is the overall, lifetime tax burden.

- **Regular 401(k), 403(b), or 457(b) governmental plan:** Generally, individuals with a relatively short period of time until retirement, or who expect that their marginal tax rate will be lower in retirement, will benefit more from a regular, pre-tax qualified retirement plan.

- **Designated Roth account:** Younger individuals with more years until retirement and those who anticipate that their marginal tax rate will rise in retirement will generally benefit more from a designated Roth account. The fact that contributions to a designated Roth account are after-tax may cause current cash-flow problems for some individuals. Higher income participants may find that taxable income will be higher with a designated Roth account than with a

63

regular pre-tax plan, potentially reducing tax breaks such as the child tax credit or AMT exemption.

- **Both:** Some individuals may choose to contribute to both types of plan, to provide flexibility in retirement.

SEEK PROFESSIONAL GUIDANCE

Because of the complexities involved, the guidance of tax andfinancial professionals is strongly recommended.

APPENDIX II

ROTH IRAs

The Roth IRA differs from the traditional IRA in that contributions are never deductible and, if certain requirements are met, account distributions are free of federal income tax.1

FUNDING A ROTH IRA

Annual contributions: A Roth IRA may be established and funded at any time between January 1 of the current year, up to and including the date an individual's federal income tax return is due, (generally April 15 of the following year), not including extensions.

CONVERSION OF A TRADITIONAL IRA ACCOUNT

A traditional IRA may be converted to a Roth IRA, with the conversion being a taxable event. For the year of conversion the taxpayer must include in gross income previously deducted contributions plus net earnings (or minus net losses). For individual retirement annuities, gross income is generally increased by the fair market value of the contract on the date of conversion (through a redesignation) or distribution (if held inside an IRA). If a retirement annuity is completely surrendered, the cash received is the amount includable in income. Any 10% penalty tax for early withdrawal is waived. However, if a taxpayer withdraws amounts from the Roth IRA within five years of the conversion, the 10% penalty tax will apply to those amounts deemed to be part of the conversion, unless an exception applies.

Prior to 2018, a taxpayer who converted a traditional IRA to a Roth IRA could "undo" the transaction and "recharacterize" the converted funds, moving them back into a traditional IRA.

However, for tax years beginning in 2018, the Tax Cuts and Jobs Act of 2017 (TCJA), permanently repealed the ability to recharacterize a Roth conversion back to a traditional IRA.

TCJA did not repeal the ability of a taxpayer to convert a Roth IRA to a traditional IRA and then recharacterize the converted funds, moving them back into a Roth IRA

ROLLOVERS FROM A QUALIFIED PLAN

Distributions from qualified retirement plans, IRC Sec. 457(b) governmental plans, and IRC Sec. 403(b) plans may also be rolled over to a Roth IRA. These conversions are taxable events, with gross income for the year of conversion being increased by previously deducted contributions plus net earnings (or minus net losses).

Direct rollover from a designated Roth Account: Funds may be rolled into a regular Roth IRA from a designated Roth account that is part of a 401(k), 403(b), or 457(b) governmental plan. Such a rollover is not a taxable event and the filing status and MAGI limitations normally applicable to regular Roth contributions do not apply.

MILITARY DEATH PAYMENTS

Under the provisions of the Heroes Earnings Assistance and Relief Tax Act of 2008, an individual who receives a military death gratuity and/or a payment under the Servicemembers' Group Life Insurance (SGLI) program may contribute to a Roth IRA an amount no greater than the sum of any military death gratuity and SGLI payment. Such a contribution is considered a qualified rollover contribution and must be made within one year of receiving the death gratuity or insurance payment. The annual dollar contribution

limit and income-based phase-out of the dollar contribution limit do not apply to such contributions.

TYPE OF ARRANGEMENTS PERMITTED

There are currently two types of Roth IRAs.

- **Individual retirement accounts:** Trusts or custodial accounts with a corporate trustee or custodian.
- **Individual retirement annuities:** Special annuities issued by a life insurance company.

CONTRIBUTION LIMITS

Limits: For 2020, an individual may contribute (but not necessarily deduct) the lesser of $6,000 or 100% of compensation[2] for the year. For a married couple, an additional $5,500 may be

---

[2] "Compensation" includes taxable wages, salaries, or commissions or the net income from self-employment

contributed on behalf of a lesser earning (or nonworking) spouse, using a spousal account.

A husband and wife may contribute up to a total of $11,000, as long as their combined compensation is at least that amount.[3]

If an IRA owner is age 50 or older, he or she may contribute an additional $1,000 ($2,000 if the spouse is also age 50 or older).

Other IRAs: The contribution limits for a Roth IRA are coordinated with those of a traditional IRA; a taxpayer may not contribute more than the annual limit for that tax year into a single IRA or a combination of traditional and Roth IRAs. Excess contributions to a traditional or Roth IRA are subject to a 6% excise tax.

Contribution phase out: For 2020, the maximum contribution to a Roth IRA is phased out for single taxpayers with MAGI between

$124,300 and $139,000. For married couples filing jointly, the phase- out range is a MAGI of $196,000 to $206,000. For married

---

[3] These amounts apply to 2018. For 2017, the maximum allowable contribution was also $5,500 for a single individual and $11,000 for a married couple.

individuals filing separately, the phase-out range is a MAGI of $0 to $10,000.[4]

TAXATION OF DISTRIBUTIONS

A distribution from a Roth IRA that is a "qualified" distribution is excluded from gross income and is not subject to federal income tax. A distribution is qualified if it is made after a five-year waiting period[5] and at least one of the following requirements is met:

- after the taxpayer reaches age 59½; or
- due to the taxpayer's death; or
- because the taxpayer becomes disabled; or
- to pay for first-time-home-buyer expenses up to $10,000.

---

[4] For 2017, the phase-out ranges were: (1) MFJ – MAGI of $186,000 - $196,000 and (2) Single - $118,000 - $133,000. For those using the MFS filing status, the phase-out range is $0 - $10,000, which does not change.

[5] Generally, five years after a contribution is first made, or amounts are converted to a Roth IRA.

The earnings portion of a "non-qualified" distribution is subject to tax. To determine any taxable distribution, the funds are considered to be withdrawn in a specified order

- Any withdrawal is considered to come first from non-deductible contributions, which are not subject to tax.
- After all contributions have been withdrawn, any conversion amounts are considered next. A distribution of converted funds is not included in gross income, but may be subject to the 10% premature distribution penalty if the funds are withdrawn within five years of being converted.
- Once all contributions and conversions have been withdrawn, any remaining funds are deemed to be earnings, and, when distributed, are included in gross income.

PREMATURE DISTRIBUTIONS

If a taxable distribution is received prior to age 59½, a 10% penalty tax is added to the regular income tax due, unless one or more of the following exceptions apply:

- A distribution is made because of the death or disability of the account owner.

- A withdrawal is part of a scheduled series of substantially equal periodic payments.

- A distribution is rolled-over into another Roth IRA.

- A withdrawal is used to pay for deductible medical expenses

- The distribution is used to pay for certain qualified higher-education expenses.

- Amounts are withdrawn to pay for first-time homebuyer expenses of up to $10,000.

- In certain situations, to pay health insurance premiums for unemployed individuals.

- Distributions by certain military reservists called to active duty after 09/11/2001.

- A distribution is transferred to a Health Savings Account (HSA).

- In case of an IRS levy on the account.

OTHER DIFFERENCES

There are several other significant differences between the traditional and Roth IRAs:

Contributions after age 72: Contributions to a Roth IRA may be made even after the taxpayer has reached age 70½, as long as the taxpayer has compensation at least equal to the contribution, subject to the phase-out rules.

Distribution requirements: Roth IRAs are not subject to the mandatory required minimum distribution (RMD) rules during the life of the owner (triggered at age 72) applicable to traditional IRAs. However, there are post-death minimum distribution rules applicable to non-spousal beneficiaries who inherit a Roth account

CHARITABLE DISTRIBUTIONS

Federal income tax law provides for an exclusion from gross income of up to $100,000 for distributions made from a Roth or traditional IRA directly to a qualified charitable organization. Such a distribution counts towards the taxpayer's RMD requirements.

The IRA owner (Or beneficiary of an inherited IRA) must be at least age 70½ when the distribution is made. No charitable deduction is allowed for such a qualified charitable distribution.

TRANSFERS TO HEALTH SAVINGS ACCOUNTS (HSAs)

Federal law allows for a limited, one-time, direct transfer of funds from an IRA to an HSA. If certain requirements are met, any otherwise taxable portion of the distribution is excluded from income and the 10% early distribution penalty will not apply.

INVESTMENT ALTERNATIVES

- **Banks, savings and loans, credit unions:** Certificates of deposit in Roth IRAs are generally insured by either the FDIC or the NCUA for amounts up to $250,000. Fixed and variable rates are available. There may be stiff penalties for early withdrawal.

- **Annuities:** Traditional, fixed individual retirement annuities issued by life insurance companies can guarantee fixe monthly income at retirement and may include a disability-waiver-of-premium provision. Variable annuities do not guarantee a fixed monthly income at retirement.

- **Money market:** Yield fluctuates with the economy. Investor cannot lock in higher interest rates. It is easy to switch to other investments.

- **Mutual funds:** A wide variety of mutual funds with many investment objectives are available.

- **Zero coupon bonds:** Bonds are issued at a deep discount from face value. There are no worries about reinvesting interest payments. Zero coupon bonds are subject to inflation risk and interest rate risk.

- **Stocks:** A wide variety of investments (and risk) is possible. Losses are generally not deductible.

- **Limited partnerships:** Some limited partnerships are especially designed for qualified plans, specifically in the areas of real estate and mortgage pools.

- **Prohibited Investments or Transactions**

- **Life insurance:** Roth IRAs cannot include life insurance contracts.

- **Loans to IRA taxpayer:** Self-borrowing triggers a constructive distribution of the entire amount in an IRA.

- **Collectibles:** Purchase of art works, antiques, metals, gems, stamps, etc., will be treated as a taxable distribution. Coins issued under state law and certain U.S. gold, silver and platinum coins are exceptions. Certain kinds of bullion may be purchased.

OTHER FACTORS TO CONSIDER

- What is the yield? More frequent compounding will produce a higher return. Is the interest rate fixed or variable? If interest rates drop, a fixed rate may be better, especially if you can make future contributions at the same fixed rate. If interest rates go up, you may be able to roll the account to another Roth IRA.

- How often can you change investments? Is there a charge?

- Refunds of federal income taxes may be directly deposited into an IRA.

- Federal bankruptcy law protects assets in Roth IRA accounts, up to $1,283,025.[6] Funds rolled over from qualified plans are protected without limit.

---

[6] Effective April 1, 2016. The limit is indexed for inflation every three years.

APPENDIX III

ROTH IRA CONVERSION FACTORS TO CONSIDER

Before 2010, taxpayers[7] with a modified adjusted gross income (MAGI)[8] in excess of $100,000, or who filed their federal income tax returns using the Married Filing Separately filing status, were prohibited from converting a traditional IRA to a Roth IRA. Beginning in 2010, however, these prohibitions no longer applied.

For many individuals, the ability to convert a traditional IRA to a Roth IRA represents a significant tax planning opportunity.[9]

---

[7] The discussion here concerns federal income tax law. State or local law may differ.

[8] Modified adjusted gross income (MAGI) is a taxpayer's adjusted gross income (AGI) with certain deductions or exclusions added back. For most taxpayers, MAGI and AGI are the same.

[9] Although the discussion here focuses on traditional IRAs, the same rules apply to amounts converted from a SEP IRA or SIMPLE IRA to a Roth IRA. Funds in a SIMPLE IRA that do not meet the two-year period described in IRC Sec. 72(t)(6) may not be converted. Distributions from IRC Sec. 401(a)

PAY ME LATER OR PAY ME NOW

With a traditional IRA, and assuming certain requirements are met, contributions are deductible in the year they are made. The tax due on the contributions, and the tax due on any earnings or growth, is deferred until funds are distributed from the account, typically at retirement. From an income tax perspective, this is a "pay me later" scenario.

With a Roth IRA, contributions are never deductible; they are made with funds that have already been taxed. If certain requirements are met, both the contributions and any earnings or growth are received income-tax free when withdrawn from the account. From an income tax perspective, this is a "pay me now" scenario.

A taxpayer who elects to convert a traditional IRA to a Roth IRA has chosen to pay the income tax now rather than waiting until the future to pay it. To justify a conversion, the benefit of not paying taxes tomorrow should be greater than the cost of paying taxes today

---

qualified retirement plans, IRC Sec. 457(b) governmental plans, and IRC Sec. 403(b) plans may also be rolled over into a Roth IRA

BENEFITS OF ROTH IRAS

The benefits of holding assets in a Roth IRA can be considerable:

- **During life – tax-free income:** Assuming that certain requirements are met, including a five-taxable year waiting period after a contribution is first made to a Roth IRA for the owner, "qualified" distributions are received income-tax free.

- **At death – income-tax free to beneficiaries:** At death, the value of the Roth IRA is includable in the account owner's estate, subject to federal estate tax. A surviving spouse can treat an inherited Roth IRA as his or her own, with the proceeds being received income-tax free, and with no required minimum distributions. For non- spousal beneficiaries, and assuming that the five-year waiting period requirement has been met, the proceeds are received income-tax free. After the owner's death, however, non-spousal beneficiaries must take certain required minimum distributions.

- **No lifetime required minimum distributions:** Federal income tax law mandates that certain required minimum distributions be made from traditional IRAs, beginning when the account owner reaches age 72. For Roth IRAs, there are no minimum distribution requirements during the lifetime of the account owner.

- **No age limit on contributions:** As long as a taxpayer has "compensation" (such as wages or self-employment income), contributions may be made to a Roth IRA regardless of the taxpayer's age, subject to the modified adjusted gross income limitations.

THE COST OF CONVERSION

Converting a traditional IRA to a Roth IRA is a currently taxable event. For the year the converted assets are distributed, the taxpayer must include in gross income all previously deducted contributions, plus net earnings (or minus net losses). For individual retirement annuities, gross income is generally increased by the fair market value of the contract on the date of conversion (through a re-designation) or distribution (if held inside an IRA). If a retirement annuity is completely surrendered, the cash received is the amount includable in income. Any 10% penalty tax for early withdrawal is waived.

If a taxpayer has traditional IRA accounts that hold both deductible and non-deductible amounts, he or she may not "cherry-pick" and convert only the non-deductible contributions.[10] Instead, the value of all IRA accounts is added together and a ratio is calculated to determine the tax-free portion of any conversion.[11]

Example: Paul has a traditional IRA to which he has made

$20,000 in non-deductible contributions. This year, when he converts the account to a Roth IRA, the balance in this IRA is $30,000. Paul also has a separate IRA containing $70,000 in pre-tax contributions rolled over from a 401(k) plan with a previous employer. The total value of both accounts is $100,000. His "non-deductible" ratio is thus 20%, ($20,000 ÷ $100,000). When Paul converts the $30,000 in his non-deductible IRA, he may exclude only $6,000 (20% x $30,000) from gross income. The remaining $24,000 ($30,000 - $6,000) is includable in his gross income, subject to tax.

---

[10] Because they have already been taxed, non-deductible contributions are generally not taxable when converted from a traditional IRA to a Roth IRA.

[11] If all of the contributions to the traditional IRA were deductible, a taxpayer may elect to roll over everything, or pick and choose which accounts or portions of an account to convert.

Ryan J. Fleming, MBA, RICP, CRPC

SITUATIONS FAVORING CONVERSION TO A ROTH IRA

- **Small account values:** If the dollar amount in the traditional IRA is small, the income- tax cost to convert today would be relatively low.

- **Longer time to retirement:** A longer period of time until retirement allows for greater future growth, necessary to recoup the up-front cost of paying the tax now.

- **Cash to pay the taxes:** Where will the money come from to pay the extra taxes? It's usually better if the account owner has sufficient cash outside of the IRA to pay the tax. Could the funds used to pay the tax today provide a greater return if invested elsewhere?

- **IRA income not needed:** Some individuals have adequate retirement income from other sources, so that IRA monies are not needed to fund retirement. During the lifetime of the account owner, a Roth IRA has no minimum distribution requirements.

- **Higher future tax bracket:** If a taxpayer anticipates being in a higher tax bracket in the future, paying the tax today, at

83

lower rates, is a logical step. Being taxed at a higher marginal rate may be the result of legislative changes, having a higher taxable income, or a change in filing status, such as when a couple divorces or a spouse dies.

SITUATIONS NOT FAVORING CONVERSION

In some situations, converting a traditional IRA to a Roth IRA may not be appropriate:

- **Retirement begins soon:** If there is only a short time before retirement begins, there may not be enough time for future growth to offset the cost of paying the tax today.

- **High IRA account values:** If the dollar amount in the traditional IRA is large, the tax bill resulting from the conversion will likely be expensive; the conversion could push a taxpayer into a higher marginal tax bracket or make Social Security benefits taxable

- **No cash to pay the taxes:** A taxpayer may not have the cash outside the IRA to pay the extra tax that results from the conversion. Taking funds from the IRA to pay the increased tax reduces the amount left in the account to grow into the future. If the account owner is under age 59½ at the time these extra funds are withdrawn from the IRA, a 10% penalty on the amount not converted will likely be added to the tax bill.

- **Lower future tax rates:** If a taxpayer anticipates being in a lower tax bracket in the future, paying the tax today, at higher marginal tax rates, makes no sense.

RECHARACTERIZATION

Prior to 2018, a taxpayer who converted a traditional IRA to a Roth IRA could "undo" the transaction and "recharacterize" the converted funds, moving them back into a traditional IRA.

However, for tax years beginning in 2018, the Tax Cuts and Jobs Act of 2017 (TCJA), permanently repealed the ability to recharacterize a Roth conversion back to a traditional IRA.

SEEK PROFESSIONAL GUIDANCE

The decision to convert all or part of a traditional IRA to a Roth IRA is an individual one. A thorough analysis requires careful consideration of a number of income tax, investment, and estat planning factors, over an extended time horizon. The advice and guidance of appropriate financial, tax, and investment professionals is strongly recommended.

APPENDIX IV

IRC SEC. 72(t)(2)(A)(iv)

Generally, taxable distributions from employer-sponsored qualified retirement plans, and from traditional and Roth IRAs, made before the account owner reaches age 59½, are subject to a 10% "early" withdrawal penalty.12 One exception to this 10% penalty is for distributions taken as a series of "substantially equal periodic payments."[12]

This exception applies to distributions made, at least once a year, over the life (or life expectancy) of the participant, or over the joint lives (or joint life expectancies) of the participant and a beneficiary. The payments must continue unchanged (except for death or disability) for the longer of: (a) five years (five years from the date of the first payment), or (b) the participant reaches age 59½.

---

[12] The discussion here concerns federal income tax law. State or local law may differ. Under federal law, the 10% penalty generally applies to distributions which are includable in gross income

Otherwise, the 10% penalty will be applied retroactively and interest will be charged

CALCULATING THE SUBSTANTIALLY-EQUAL PERIODIC PAYMENT

In Notice 89-25, 11989-1, CB 662, Q&A-12 (March 20, 1989), the IRS listed three acceptable methods of calculating such a distribution:

- **Required minimum distribution (RMD):** The annual payment is determined using a method acceptable for calculating the required minimum distribution required under IRC Sec. 401(a)(9). In general, the account balance is divided by a life expectancy factor, resulting in a payment which changes from year to year.

- **Fixed amortization method:** Payment under this method is similar to the annual amount required to pay off a loan (equal to the amount in the plan at the start of distributions), at a reasonable interest rate, over the remainder of one's life. The dollar amount of the payment remains the same in each subsequent year.

- **Fixed annuitization:** An annuity factor is determined from a reasonable mortality table at an interest rate which is then reasonable for the age of the recipient of the distribution. The payment is determined for the first distribution and remains the same in each subsequent year.

REVENUE RULING 2002-6

On October 3, 2002, the IRS released Revenue Ruling 2002-62, to address questions raised by taxpayers who had begun to receive distributions under IRC Sec. 72(t)(2)(A)(iv) and who had been adversely affected by a declining stock market. This ruling contained the following key points.

- It expanded the guidance given in Q&A 12 of IRS Notice 89-25 to, among other things, incorporate into the calculation process the new life expectancy tables issued in April, 2002, with regard to required minimum distributions from IRAs and qualified plans.
- Allowed a participant who had been using either the fixed amortization method or the fixed annuitization method to make a one-time change to the RMD method.

■ Specified that if a participant who is using an acceptable method to calculate the required substantially equal periodic payments exhausts the assets in an account prior to the required time period, the "cessation of payments will not be treated as a modification of the series of payments."

The guidance provided in Revenue Ruling 2002-62 replaced the guidance of IRS Notice 89-25 for any series of payments beginning on or after January 1, 2003. If distributions began before 2003 under any method that satisfied IRC Sec. 72(t)(2)(A)(iv), a change to the required minimum distribution calculation method may be made at any time.

COMPARING THE THREE METHODS[13]

Assumptions:

Plan or IRA account balance on 12/31 of the previous year:

---

[13] The examples shown are from the IRS web site, www.irs.gov, "Retirement Plans FAQs Regarding Substantially Equal Periodic Payments," August 4, 2017.

$400,000 Age of participant in distribution year: 50 Single life expectancy at age 50: 34.2[14] Interest rate assumed: 2.98%[15] Distribution period: Single life only

Required minimum distribution method: For the current year, the annual distribution amount is calculated by dividing account balance by the participant's life expectancy.

$400,000 / 34.2 = $11,696

Fixed amortization method: Distribution amount is calculated by amortizing the account balance over the number of years of the participant's single life expectancy. The calculation is the same as in determining the payment required to pay off a loan.

$400,000 x (.0298 / (1 − (1 + .0298)^-34.2)) = $18,811

---

[14] Derived from the Single Life Table found in Reg.1.401(a)(9)-9, Q&A-1. The Uniform Lifetime Table found in Appendix A of Revenue Ruling 2002-62 or the Joint and Last Survivor table of Reg.1.401(a)(9)-9, Q&A-3 may also be used.

[15] This rate is equal to 120% of the federal mid-term rate. In these IRS examples, the rate for April 2011 is used. This value will fluctuate and changes monthly.

Fixed annuitization method: The distribution amount is equal to the account balance divided by an annuity factor that for the present value of an annuity of one dollar per year paid over the life of year-old participant. Such annuity factors are typically calculated by an actuary. In this case, the age-50 annuity factor (21.345) is based on the mortality table in Appendix B of Revenue Ruling 2002-62 and an interest rate of 2.98%.

$400,000 / 21.345 = $18,740

Method	Annual Withdrawal
Required minimum distribution	$11,696
Fixed amortization	$18,811
Fixed annuitization	$18,740

APPENDIX V

CASH VALUE LIFE INSURANCE

ACCUMULATING FUNDS TO MEET SAVINGS GOALS

Saving money to reach an accumulation goal is a problem many of us face. Some goals, such as retirement or a college fund for a child, are long-term savings goals. Many of us also have shorter-term savings goals such as a vacation or a Christmas or holiday fund.

Whatever the objective, the basic problem is the same, i.e. where to put money aside to reach a particular savings goal. For many short-term goals, a savings account at a local bank or credit union is a popular choice. For college funding, Coverdell IRAs or IRC Sec. 529 plans are often used. For retirement savings, many individual depend on Individual Retirement Accounts (IRAs) or employer-sponsored retirement plans such as an IRC Sec. 401(k) plan.

An additional option for long-term savings, one that is sometimes overlooked, is using a cash value life insurance policy.

WHAT IS CASH VALUE LIFE INSURANCE?

Life insurance comes in two basic variations, "term" insurance and "cash value" life insurance. Term life insurance can be compared to auto insurance. Protection is provided for a specified period of time or "term." No death benefits are paid unless the insured dies during the term the policy is in force. If the insured lives beyond the term period, the policy generally expires with nothing returned to the policy owner.

In addition to providing a death benefit, "cash value" life insurance also provides for the tax- deferred accumulation of money inside the policy. These funds can be used by the policy owner while the insured is alive to provide the resources for needs such as funding a college education, making improvements to the home, or starting a business. When the policy owner uses the cash values to meet such needs, he or she is said to have used the "living benefits" of a cash value life insurance policy.

WHEN TO CONSIDER CASH VALUE LIFE INSURANCE

Using a cash value life insurance policy to reach a saving goal works best in certain situations:

- **A need for life insurance death benefit** apart from the need for additional savings, an individual should have a need for the death benefit that life insurance provides. For example, such a need exists when an individual has a dependent spouse or children who would suffer economically if the individual died. Someone with a large estate might need additional cash at death to pay estate and other taxes as well as final expenses.

- **Other savings aren't enough:** Because of limitations in federal tax law,[16] other accumulation vehicles might not allow enough money to be put aside to meet a particular savings goal.

- **Time frame:** Ideally, there should be at least 10 to 15 years between today and the time the money will be needed.

---

[16] The discussion here concerns federal income tax law. State or local tax law may vary widely.

Because of mortality expenses and other policy charges, significant cash value accumulations are generally deferred until a policy has been in force for a number of years. Additionally, federal income tax law affects the design of cash value life insurance policies as well as the taxation of cash value withdrawals in the early years a policy is in force

- **Insurable:** The insured needs to be healthy enough to have a policy issued on his or her life.

- **An ongoing obligation:** Cash value life insurance policies tend to have a higher premium cost than comparable term life policies. Paying the premiums over a number of years represents an ongoing financial obligation, to both keep the policy in force and achieve the savings goal.

INCOME TAX CONSIDERATIONS

There are a number of income tax issues to keep in mind when considering any life insurance policy. The death benefit payable under a life insurance contract because of the death of the insured is generally received income-tax free. Federal income taxation of life insurance "living benefits" is more complicated:

- **Tax-deferred growth:** The growth of cash value inside a life insurance policy is tax- deferred.

- **Cost recovery rule:** Amounts withdrawn from a cash- value life insurance contract are included in gross income (and become subject to tax) only when they exceed the policy owner's basis in the policy. This basis is also known as the "investment in the contract." This effectively treats withdrawals from the policy first as a non-taxable return of premium and secondly as taxable income.

- **Investment in the contract:** The total of all premium paid less any policy dividends and any other prior tax-free distributions received.

- **Policy dividends:** Some "participating" life policies pay what are termed "dividends." Such dividends are a return of a portion of the policy owner's previously paid premiums. Policy dividends are not taxable until they exceed the owner's basis in the life insurance contract.

- **Policy loans:** Some cash value life insurance policies allow the policy owner to borrow at interest a portion of the accumulated cash value. While a policy is in force, policy loans are generally not taxable. However, if a policy is surrendered with a loan outstanding, taxable income will result to the extent that the unpaid loan amount exceeds the owner's basis in the contract.

- **Modified Endowment Contracts (MECs):** Some life insurance policies – primarily because there are large premium payments in the early years of the contract – are termed "Modified Endowment Contracts," or MECs. Under federal income tax law, distributions from a policy considered to be a MEC are treated differently than distributions from non- MEC policies. Withdrawals from a MEC (including a policy loan) will first be taxed as current income until all of the policy earnings have been taxed. If the owner is under age 59½, a 10% penalty also applies, unless the payments are due to disability or are annuity type payments. Once all policy earnings have been distributed (and taxed), any further withdrawals are treated as a non-taxable return of premium.

ACCESSING THE CONTRACT'S CASH VALUES

When the time comes to use the accumulated cash values, withdrawals from the policy should be done in such a way as to avoid current income taxation (to the extent possible) and keep the policy in force.

- **Withdrawal to basis:** Initially a policy owner can take withdrawals (partial policy surrenders) until he or she has withdrawn an amount equal to the basis in the policy.

- **Switching to policy loans:** Once the basis has been withdrawn, the policy owner then begins using non- taxable policy loans. The interest payable on these policy loans is typically much less than a loan from a commercial bank or credit union.

- **A combination:** A policy owner can also use a combination of withdrawals and policy loans.

- **Caveats:** There are a number of issues that a policy owner needs to keep in mind:

- Withdrawals reduce the death benefit available under the policy

- If an insured dies with a policy loan outstanding, the policy's death benefit is reduced by the amount of the loan balance.

- Excessive use of withdrawals and policy loans can result in the policy lapsing. Such a lapse can result in unexpected, negative tax results as well as the loss of a valuable financial asset.

A MULTI-FUNCTION TOOL

Used appropriately, cash value life insurance can serve as financial tool with multiple uses. It can be used, in conjunction with more traditional savings vehicles, as a way to accumulate funds for long- term savings goals. At the same time the policy can, if the insured dies, provide a death benefit when the funds are most needed.

SEEK PROFESSIONAL GUIDANCE

Determining the appropriate amount of life insurance, the best type of policy to meet the needs of an individual's specific situation, and planning when and how to access a policy's cash values can be complex and confusing. The advice and guidance of trained insurance, tax, and other financial professionals is strongly recommended.

APPENDIX VI

LIFE INSURANCE– LTC COMBINATION POLICIES

Providing for health care is a key part of retirement planning. For most Americans age 65 and over, the federal government's Medicare program, and its various components, provides most of the resources to take care of a typical retiree's health care needs.

One health care need that is only minimally covered by Medicare is that of long-term care (LTC). LTC is the term used to describe a variety of maintenance or "custodial" services required by individuals who are chronically disabled, ill, or infirm. Depending on individual needs, LTC may include nursing home care, assisted living, home health care, or adult day care.

Not everyone will need LTC in retirement. For those that do, LTC is expensive. In 2017, for example, the national median cost for a resident in an assisted living facility was $45,000 per year; the national median cost for a semi-private nursing home room was

$85,755 per year.[17] The problem, then, is how to pay for an expensive need that may, or may not, occur.

One answer has been that of a stand-alone, long-term care insurance policy. Should the need arise, a LTC policy can furnish some or all of the resources needed to pay for care. LTC insurance can be expensive, however, and most policies allow for the possibility of future rate increases. Plus, if an individual uses few (or none) of a policy's benefits, there is a sense that the money was not well spent.

One alternative to a traditional LTC insurance policy is that of a "combination" policy that links a cash-value life insurance policy with a tax-qualified, long-term care benefit. These combination policies take advantage of federal[18] income tax law which allows for payment of "accelerated death benefits," up to the policy's death benefit, should the insured need long- term care. If LTC services are required, the policy death benefit can be used to help pay these costs. If LTC services are not needed, or only a portion of the death benefit is used to pay LTC expenses, any remaining policy death benefit (less

---

[17] Source: The Genworth 2017 Cost of Care Summary, page 2.

[18] The discussion here concerns federal income tax law. State of local income tax law may differ.

any policy loans) passes to beneficiaries named by the insured. Such a combination policy is most appropriate when there is a need for both life insurance and long-term care protection.

- **Long-term care "riders":** In return for paying an additional premium, a "rider" can be added to a life insurance policy which allows the insurance carrier to advance the policy's death benefit to the insured, if long-term care is required. With some policies, a second rider can be added to increase the total dollar amount available to pay for LTC services, beyond the policy's original death benefit.

- **Benefit "triggers":** Under federal law, tax-free, accelerated death benefits can be paid from the policy when the insured is considered to be either "terminally ill" (death is expected within 24 months) or "chronically ill." For long-term care purposes,[19] an insured is considered to be chronically ill when he or she is either (1) expected to be unable to perform for 90 days two of six activities of daily living (eating, toileting, transferring, bathing, dressing, and maintaining continence), or (2) suffers from a cognitive impairment such

---

[19] See IRC. Sec. 7702(b).

as Alzheimer's, dementia, or Parkinson's disease. With some policies, a more restrictive definition requires the underlying chronic condition to be permanent.

- **Elimination period:** Once the insured is determined to qualify, long-term care payments can begin after a waiting, or "elimination" period, which can range from 60- 100 days. The elimination period usually only has to be satisfied one time.

- **Monthly LTC benefit amount:** The monthly LTC benefit is a set percentage of the total death benefit, typically selected by the policy owner when the policy is purchased. The table below shows the payment amount and length of time for a hypothetical policy with a $100,000 death benefit:

Payout Percentage	Exemption Amount	Payout Length
1%	$1,000 per month	100 months
2%	$2,000 per month	50 months
3%	$3,000 per month	33 months
4%	$4,000 per month	25 months
5%	$5,000 per month	20 months

- **Effect of LTC payments on policy death benefit:** As LTC benefits are paid out, the policy's death benefit is reduced dollar-for-dollar.

- **Indemnity vs. actual expenses:** Some policies pay benefits on an indemnity or cash basis, meaning that once payments begin the monthly payment is the same regardless of the dollar amount of LTC expenses incurred. Policies that pay benefits on an expense basis pay the lesser of the monthly benefit or the actual LTC expenses incurred. If LTC expenses are less than the normal monthly payment, any unused balance is held over, potentially extending the benefit period.

- **Paying for the policy:** In many cases, a life insurance policy with LTC benefits is funded with a large, single premium. A few policies are paid through periodic premium payments. If appropriate, an existing cash-value life insurance may be exchanged tax- free for a new combination policy.

- **Underwriting:** Some policies, typically those funded with a large, single premium, use a streamlined, simplified underwriting process, with no medical exam. Other policies may require a medical exam and a complete health history.

- **Taxability of benefits:** Depending on the type of policy, long-term care benefits are received income-tax free under either IRC Sec. 101(g) or IRC Sec. 7702B.

- **Rate guarantees:** With many life insurance policies, because the death benefit is a pre- defined amount, the premiums are often guaranteed not to change. With a few types of life insurance, the premium rates may increase under certain conditions, but normally within a specified range.

- **Guaranteed return of premium:** Certain single-premium policies provide for a return of the premium paid (within a specified period of time) if the insured decides not to keep the policy. Life insurance policies which are paid for through periodic payments typically do not have this feature

- **Residual death benefit:** In some instance, a policy may include a "residual" death benefit. If this feature is included, even though the policy's death benefits are exhausted through LTC benefit payments, the policy will still pay a small amount (typically 5% - 10% of the initial death benefit) at the insured's death. This benefit allows the survivors to pay for funeral and other final expenses.

OTHER FACTORS TO CONSIDER

There are a number of other factors to keep in mind when considering a life insurance-LTC combination policy:

- **Not considered state "partnership" LTC policies:** Life-insurance-LTC combination policies generally do not qualify as state "partnership" LTC policies. An insured individual with a partnership LTC policy can keep a much larger dollar amount of assets, while still qualifying for Medicaid, once the partnership LTC policy benefits are exhausted. Normally, an individual must be nearly destitute before Medicaid will pay for long-term care.

- **Effect of inflation:** Over time, the cost of LTC, like many other things that we buy, will increase. Since it may be many years in the future before long-term care is needed, consider a combination policy that offers a cost-of-living (COLI) rider. Without such a rider, there is a risk that a policy's LTC benefits will not keep up with increases in the cost of long-term care. Generally, once a policy is in force, the death benefit does not increase. Certain types of policies (variable life, variable universal life) have a death benefit that may increase, depending on investment results.

- **Most funded with a large, single premium:** Most life insurance-LTC combination policies are funded with a large, single premium payment. In many instances, a minimum of $25,000 - $75,000 is required to purchase a significant LTC benefit amount.

- **Is this the right tool?** A combination life insurance- LTC combination may not be the right tool if, for example, the insured is already covered by adequate life insurance. If there is a potential need for additional retirement income, a deferred annuity-LTC combination may be a better fit. For some individuals, a stand-alone LTC policy is more appropriate.

SEEK PROFESSIONAL GUIDANCE

One key part of a well-prepared retirement plan is looking ahead to the possible need for long-term care. The advice and guidance of trained financial and insurance professionals, in sorting out the various options for meeting this need, is strongly recommended.